SCIENCE Q&A

LIFE
SCIENCE

Cavendish
Square
New York

Published in 2016 by Cavendish Square Publishing, LLC
243 5th Avenue, Suite 136, New York, NY 10016

© 2016 Brown Bear Books Ltd

First Edition

Website: cavendishsq.com

CPSIA Compliance Information: Batch #WS15CSQ

Library of Congress Cataloging-in-Publication Data

Life science / edited by Tim Harris.
p. cm. — (Science Q&A)
Includes index.
ISBN 978-1-50260-622-8 (hardcover) ISBN 978-1-50260-621-1 (paperback)
ISBN 978-1-50260-623-5 (ebook)
1. Life sciences — Juvenile literature. I. Harris, Tim. II. Title.

QH309.2 H37 2015
570—d23

For Brown Bear Books Ltd:
Editors: Tracey Kelly, Dawn Titmus, Tim Harris
Designer: Mary Walsh
Design Manager: Keith Davis
Editorial Director: Lindsey Lowe
Children's Publisher: Anne O'Daly
Picture Manager: Sophie Mortimer

Picture Credits:
T=Top, C=Center, B=Bottom, L=Left, R=Right

Front Cover : All pictures Shutterstock/Thinkstock.
Inside: Science Photo Library: Anthony Mercieca 6tr, Philippe Psaila 7tr; Shutterstock: 5br, 6tl, 18tr, 22tl, Rich Carey 6bl, Tatiana Gladskikh 10bl, Torsten Lorenz 7bl, Maisna 4bl, 26tl, Xavier Marchant 26b, Boris Pamikov 19bl, Pete Saloutos 11tl, Sportgraphic 5tl, 10tl; Thinkstock: Hemera 14tl, iStockphoto 15tr, 19tr, 22bl, 26tr, Photos.com 23t, 27bl, Pixland 14bl, Stockbyte 1, 18tl; U.S. Fish and Wildlife Service: 23bl, 27tr.

Brown Bear Books has made every attempt to contact the copyright holder.
If you have any information please contact licensing@brownbearbooks.co.uk

Printed in the United States of America

CONTENTS

INTRODUCTION

Life science seeks to understand how humans, animals, and plants are created and how they function. It also studies the way in which each living thing interacts with others in its environment.

If you are reading this book, you are alive and have things in common with every other living organism on Earth. Throughout Earth's history, life forms have adapted to their environments in special ways. For instance, people and animals adapt to the climate in which they live; plants produce flowers at the times of year when the animals that pollinate them are active. Humans, animals, and plants form a huge food web, where each species is dependent on the others.

Have you ever looked at your hands and wondered how they work? Or considered what makes your heart beat? The human body is amazingly complex. Here, you will learn the

◀ This tree frog is a cold-blooded amphibian, as are toads, newts, and salamanders.

The human body is an amazing machine. Its bones, joints, and muscles work together to help us excel at sports such as running and jumping.

basics of how the body functions, from the tiniest cells to systems for the nerves, circulation, digestion, and breathing; from bones of the skeleton, to joints, muscles, and skin—the largest organ of the body. You will learn how each of the five senses— sight, hearing, smell, taste, and touch—is a finely tuned mechanism adapted to help us thrive.

Humans share Earth's land and oceans with a vast number of other living things: vertebrates such as mammals, birds, fish, and sea creatures; and invertebrates such as earthworms, insects, and spiders, which make up an astonishing 97 percent of all species. But living creatures need to eat, and without plants, none would survive. You will discover all about the life cycle of a plant, and how food chains and webs support life as we know it.

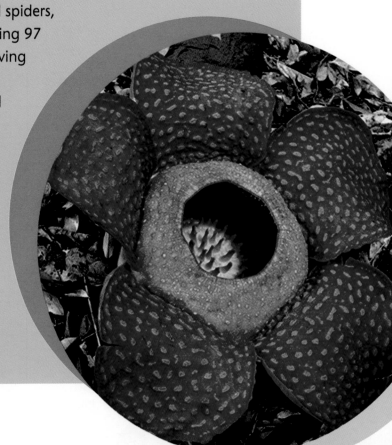

▶ The Rafflesia plant is a parasite: it gets its food from the plant it grows on.

SCIENCE OF LIFE

The science of living things (organisms) is called biology. It studies how they work, their structure, and the way they interact with other life forms.

All living things—from animals and plants to simple bacteria—are made of cells. Most cells are so small that they can be seen only under a powerful microscope. Some organisms, such as bacteria, consist of just a single cell, while others have billions of cells.

All organisms need energy to live. Animals get energy from food. Green plants and some small life forms get their energy from sunshine, through photosynthesis. Organisms create new individuals of the same type to replace those that die, a process called reproduction.

▲ **People who study biology are called biologists. Here, a biologist is checking the health of a chick.**

As they get older, animals and plants generally grow and change shape. For instance, an acorn looks nothing like the mature oak tree that will eventually grow from it.

◀ **To find out whether global warming is killing corals, biologists sometimes take photographs of them.**

▶ This biologist, high in the canopy of a tree, is collecting invertebrates in a net. He is looking for new species.

Adapt to Survive

All forms of life experience changes in their environment. If they are to survive, they must be able to sense changes and respond to them. So, for example, a bird that spends the summer months in the tundra of Siberia can sense the shortening days in the fall. It responds by building up its fat reserves, so it can make the long flight south to warmer places. If it did not do this, it would starve during the winter.

Likewise, plants produce flowers at the times of year when those animals that pollinate them—usually insects—are active. If they flowered at a different time of year, they would not be pollinated and so would not be able to reproduce.

Who Does What?

The science of life is divided into many fields. Biologists who study plants are called botanists, and those who study animals are called zoologists.

Some zoologists study particular types of animals. For instance, herpetologists study amphibians and reptiles, and ornithologists study birds.

Some biologists study specific parts of animals. Biochemists study chemical reactions in plants and animals. Geneticists study genes, which determine the qualities that organisms inherit from their parents. Ecologists study how life forms relate to each other and to their environment.

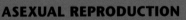

ASEXUAL REPRODUCTION
The two kinds of reproduction are asexual and sexual. In organisms that reproduce asexually, such as slime molds (left), the offspring come from a single parent. The offspring inherit the genes of that parent only. Single-celled life forms such as bacteria and many plants and fungi reproduce in this way.

GENERAL INFORMATION

● In organisms that reproduce sexually, the offspring come from two parents, so they inherit genes from both. Animals reproduce sexually, and most plants can reproduce sexually or asexually.

● Species that are able to adapt more quickly to changes in their environment have a better chance of survival.

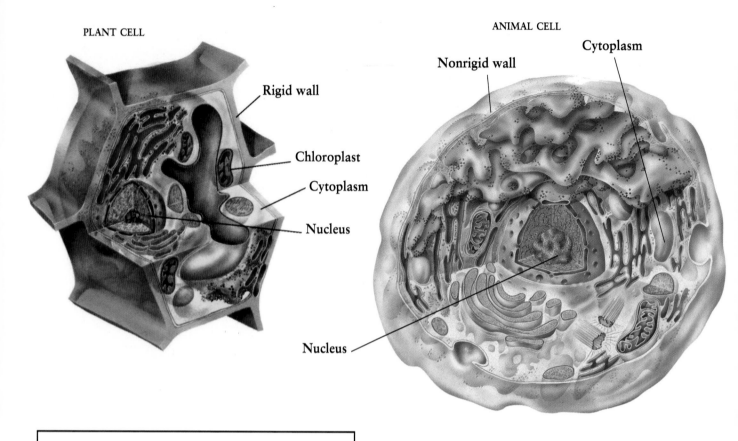

PLANT CELL

Rigid wall

Chloroplast

Cytoplasm

Nucleus

Nucleus

ANIMAL CELL

Nonrigid wall

Cytoplasm

Q Why do animals of the
same species fight?

A Animals fight others of their species for
several reasons. They may be arguing
over territory or the right to be leader of their
herd. Although many animals have powerful
weapons, such as teeth, horns, or claws, few
are ever killed in these contests. These two
klipspringer antelopes are jabbing at each
other with their sharp horns.

Q What is a cell?

A A cell (above) is the basic building block of
almost every living thing. Plant cells have a
rigid wall made from a material called cellulose.
Animal cells do not have a rigid wall. Inside all
cells is a fluid called cytoplasm, containing the
nucleus and other small bodies. The nucleus is the
cell's control center. The chloroplasts in plant cells
help trap the energy from sunlight. The energy is
then used to turn carbon dioxide and water into
food for the plant.

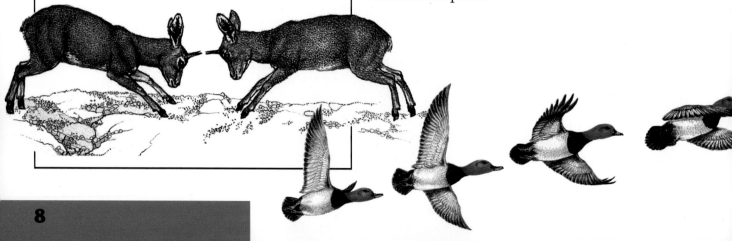

Q How do plants make seeds?

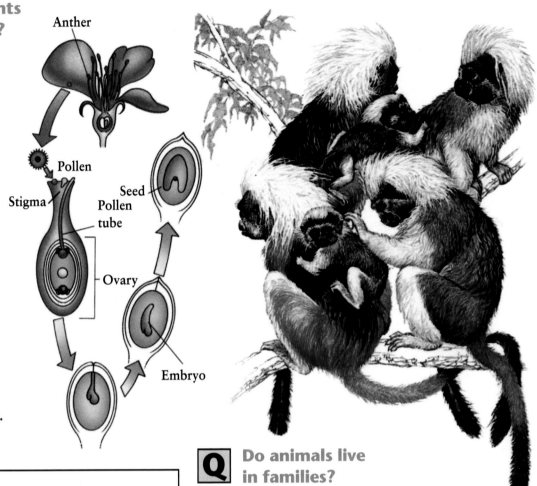

Anther

Pollen

Stigma

Seed
Pollen
tube

Ovary

Embryo

A Plants have male and female parts that join together to make seeds. A pollen grain travels from the male anther of one flower to the female stigma of another (right). The pollen is usually carried by an insect or the wind. It fertilizes an egg in the ovary, which becomes an embryo and then a seed. The seed will grow into a new plant.

Q How do racing pigeons find their way home?

A Racing pigeons and many other species of birds probably use more than one way of navigating. They can find their direction from the position of the sun by day and the stars by night. They can also detect changes in the Earth's magnetic field as they fly over it. This tells them whether they are flying north, south, east, or west. Some birds find their way by smell.

Q Do animals live in families?

A Some animals live together in herds or flocks, but others live in small family groups. This is a family of tamarin monkeys (above). The older brothers and sisters carry and help groom the babies.

Q How do birds fly?

A These pictures (below) show a duck beating its wings once as it flies. The downstroke (left) lifts the bird up and propels it forward. On the upstroke (right), the feathers are opened to let air through.

HUMAN BODY

The human body is an amazing living machine. It is made up of bones, muscles, organs, water, and lots of chemicals, all working in perfect harmony.

▼ Babies grow quickly if fed nutritional food. Mother's breast milk is recommended for the first six months of a baby's life. It is easy for the baby to digest and has the right quantities of nutrients. Breast milk also helps build the baby's immune system.

The cell is the basic unit of the human body—as it is with all other living things. Most cells join with other cells to make tissue. There are four main types of tissue: Epithelial tissue covers the body's surface; connective tissue helps join parts of the body; muscle tissue makes movement possible; and nervous tissue carries nerve signals.

Skeleton

Different kinds of tissues are combined in the body. The skeleton forms a bony structure that supports the body, provides attachments for muscles, and

Outer covering protects nerve bundles

Bundle of nerve axons

▲ Axons, or nerve fibers, carry electrical impulses from one part of the body to another.

protects delicate organs. There are 206 bones in an adult human's body. Of these, twenty-nine are in the skull, which surrounds and protects the brain. The rib bones protect the lungs. The spinal cord, one of the key parts of the nervous system, is protected by the backbone, or spine, which is actually a series of twenty-six small bones called vertebrae. Each arm has a humerus, a radius, and an ulna bone, to which muscles are attached. Each leg has

◄ There are more than six hundred muscles in the human body. Athletes use many of them when hurdling.

GENERAL INFORMATION

● A healthy body needs the right kind of carbohydrates to produce energy and for the vitamins and minerals they contain. These are called complex carbohydrates and are found in vegetables and whole-grain bread.

● The human body also needs proteins to build, maintain, and replace tissues such as muscles and organs, and red blood cells. Lean red meat, chicken, fish, dairy products, eggs, nuts, and lentils are good sources of protein.

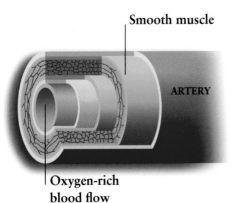

Connective tissue — Smooth muscle

VEIN

Valve controls flow of blood

Smooth muscle

ARTERY

Oxygen-rich blood flow

▲ Veins carry oxygen-poor blood to the lungs, while arteries carry oxygen-rich blood from the lungs.

a femur, or thigh bone, a tibia, and a fibula. There are twenty-seven bones in each hand and twenty-six to twenty-eight bones in each foot.

Muscles

The body has more than six hundred muscles, which move different parts of the body. There are three main types of muscles. Skeletal muscles are joined directly to bones and move arms, legs, and other body parts. They are attached to the bones by hard, ropelike tissues called tendons.

The walls of the heart are made of cardiac muscle. This is called involuntary muscle because it works without us thinking about it. The third type is smooth muscle, which is not attached to bones and does things such as move food through the digestive system.

GLANDS

Glands are tissues that secrete a variety of important substances. There are two kinds: exocrine glands and endocrine glands. The salivary glands (which produce saliva to begin the digestion of food) are exocrine glands. So is the liver, the second-largest organ after the skin. The pancreas is also an exocrine gland. It controls the level of sugar in the blood. Endocrine glands release chemical messages, or hormones, into the bloodstream. One example is the pituitary gland, which controls the water balance inside the body.

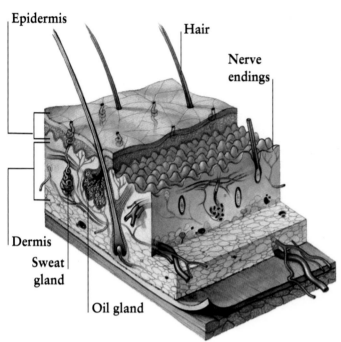

Epidermis

Hair

Nerve endings

Dermis

Sweat gland

Oil gland

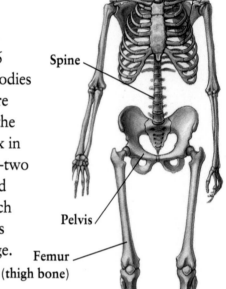

Collarbone

Skull

Rib cage

Spine

Pelvis

Femur (thigh bone)

Tibia (shinbone) and fibula

Q How many bones do we have?

A Humans have 206 bones in their bodies (right). There are twenty-nine in the skull, twenty-six in the spine, thirty-two in each arm, and thirty-one in each leg. Other bones form the rib cage.

Q What is the skin for?

A The skin (above) is the protective outer covering of our body. It contains nerve endings, which detect pain; sweat glands, which keep the body cool; and hair. It also prevents the body from losing too much water.

Q How do muscles work?

A There are more than six hundred muscles in the body (right). Most of them move parts of the body or help it to stay upright. Muscles cannot push, they can only pull. Many of them work in pairs, attached to bones by tendons. One muscle tightens and becomes shorter, pulling the bone after it. If it relaxes, and the other muscle tightens, the bone moves back.

Neck muscles turn head

Upper arm muscles bend and straighten elbow

Chest muscles used in breathing

Q What is inside a bone?

A Bones are not solid. They have a strong outer layer of compact bone, with lightweight, spongy bone inside. In the center is the soft marrow, which makes new red cells for the blood.

Blood vessel

Compact bone

Spongy bone

What are veins and arteries?

 When blood leaves the lungs, it carries oxygen. This blood travels along vessels called arteries. The body absorbs the oxygen, and the blood travels back to the heart through veins (below).

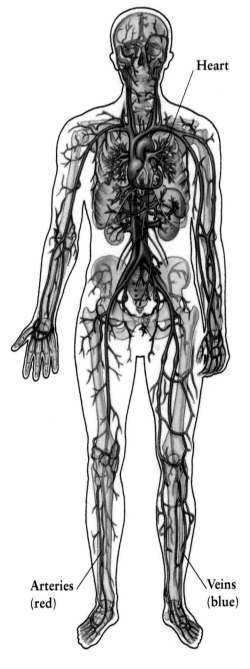

Heart

Arteries (red)

Veins (blue)

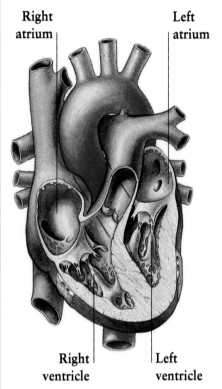

Right atrium

Left atrium

Right ventricle

Left ventricle

 **How does the heart work?**

The heart is a muscular pump. Oxygen-rich blood from the lungs enters the left atrium of the heart and is pumped to the organs. Veins carry the blood back to the right side of the heart. The blood enters the right atrium and is then pumped back to the lungs.

Q **How do our joints work?**

A Joints are the places where bones move against each other. Shoulders and hips have ball and socket joints. These allow movement in any direction. Elbows have hinge joints, which allow them to move backward and forward. A pivot joint allows the head to turn sideways.

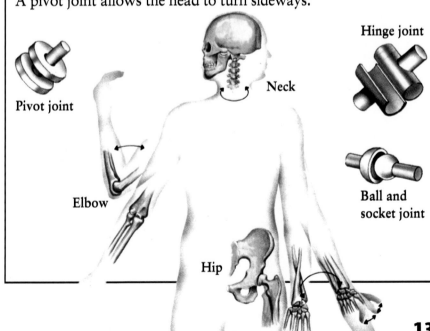

Pivot joint

Neck

Hinge joint

Elbow

Ball and socket joint

Hip

13

SENSES AND ORGANS

The human body has lots of different organs, each of which has a special job. Without any one of them, the body would not work properly.

KEY FACTS

Brain: Although it amounts to only 2 percent of the body's weight, it uses 20 percent of the body's oxygen intake.

Blood vessels: If connected, the lungs' blood vessels would stretch 1,500 miles (2,400 km).

Sense of smell: The human nose can recognize about fifty thousand different scents.

Skin: The outer layer of skin cells is shed and regrown every twenty-seven days on average.

Without some organs, the body would not be able to function at all. The body's organs include the heart, lungs, brain, liver, stomach, and small intestine. The skin is the largest organ. It protects the body from air, water, dirt, and bacteria. Organs such as the eyes and ears give us our senses.

Lungs and Heart

Air passes from the nose and mouth and through the windpipe, or trachea, which branches into the two lungs. Thousands of tiny tubes called bronchioles carry air to

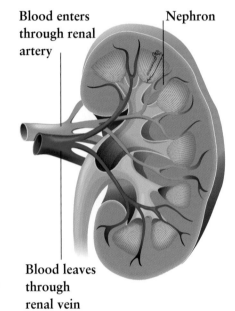

Blood enters through renal artery

Nephron

Blood leaves through renal vein

▲ A cross section through a human kidney. There are at least one million nephrons, which filter waste from the blood.

alveoli, where oxygen passes into tiny blood vessels called capillaries. This oxygen is vital for the body to function. Waste carbon dioxide passes the other way, from the capillaries to the alveoli and then out of the body. This whole process is called the respiratory system. It works in harmony with the blood circulatory system.

The heart is a muscular pump at the center of the circulatory system, which carries blood to all parts of the body. The heart pushes oxygen-rich blood from the lungs around

◀ Our senses are important for seeing, hearing, smelling, tasting, and touching.

the body in arteries. It pumps blood that lacks oxygen through veins and back to the lungs. There, the blood absorbs more oxygen.

Digestive Organs

Food must pass through the digestive system before the body can use it for energy. Food ends up in the stomach after being chewed and swallowed. Chemicals in the stomach convert the food into a soupy substance that passes to the small intestine. There, it is turned into sugars and fatty acids by juices sent from the liver and pancreas. The digested materials pass into the bloodstream to help the body function. Undigested food passes into the large intestine and out of

THE SENSE OF SOUND
Our eyes give us the sense of sight, and our ears give us the sense of sound. Our ears receive sound waves, which are passed from the outer ear to the inner ear. There, they are changed into signals to be sent along the cochlear nerve to the brain. The brain interprets these messages as loud, soft, or low- or high-pitched sounds.

the body. The liver makes safe the toxins that are produced in the large intestine.

The human body has two kidneys. They filter waste products from the blood and excrete them as

urine. The kidneys maintain the body's water and mineral balances. The kidneys also help control blood pressure and produce red blood cells.

The Nervous System

The brain controls the nervous system. This is made up of the nerves, spinal cord, and all the sense organs. Messages from the brain are sent along the nerves to get the body to do things. The sense organs pick up information about the environment—sights, sounds, odors, and temperature—and pass it back to the brain.

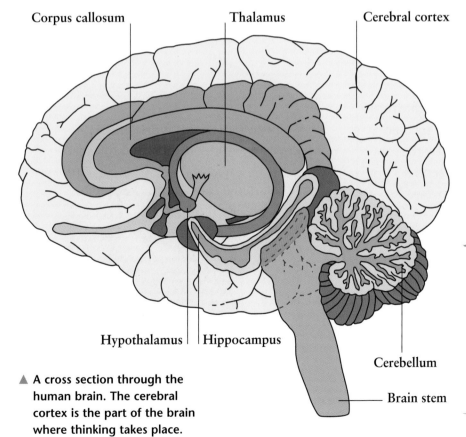

Corpus callosum   Thalamus   Cerebral cortex

Hypothalamus | Hippocampus

Cerebellum

Brain stem

▲ A cross section through the human brain. The cerebral cortex is the part of the brain where thinking takes place.

GENERAL INFORMATION

● The body has a single liver, which processes digested food from the intestines, combats infections, and controls the levels of fats, amino acids, and glucose in the blood.

Q How do we breathe?

 A Our bodies need oxygen, which they get from air breathed into the lungs. The lungs are made to expand by a big muscle called the diaphragm and smaller muscles fixed to the ribs. The diaphragm pushes downward, while the other muscles lift up the rib cage. This draws air down into the lungs, where the oxygen is absorbed into the bloodstream (right).

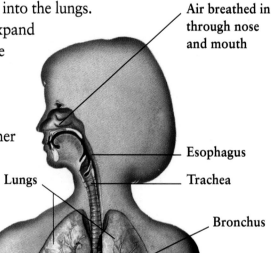

Air breathed in through nose and mouth

Esophagus

Trachea

Lungs

Bronchus

Diaphragm

Q Where does our food go?

A After the teeth chew the food, it is swallowed and goes down the esophagus into the stomach (below). It is mixed with digestive juices, which break it down. In the small intestine, nutrients from the food are absorbed. Waste matter leaves the body through the anus.

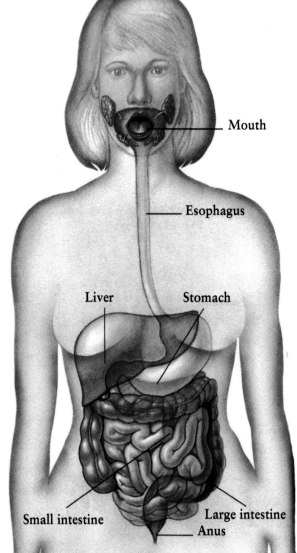

Mouth

Esophagus

Liver

Stomach

Small intestine

Large intestine

Anus

Q How do our eyes see?

 A When we look at something, light from it enters our eyes. The light is focused on the retina at the back of the eye by the lens. The optic nerves in the retina send a message to the brain, enabling us to "see."

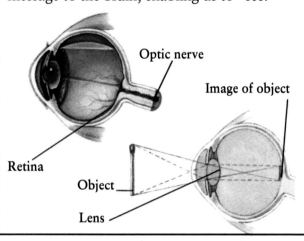

Optic nerve

Image of object

Retina

Object

Lens

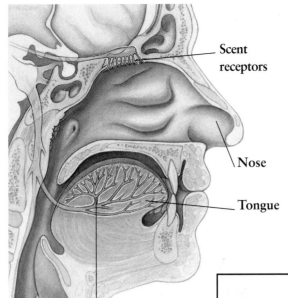

Scent receptors

Nose

Tongue

Taste receptors

Q How do we taste and smell?

A In the upper part of the nose there are tiny scent receptors (left). When we sniff, molecules in the air are carried to these receptors. They sense what we are smelling. The tongue is covered with about nine thousand taste receptors, or taste buds. These sense what we are tasting. The taste buds are grouped in special areas on the tongue. Sweetness is tasted at the front, saltiness and sourness at the sides, and bitterness at the back.

Q How do our ears work?

A The outer ear collects sound waves, which pass through the eardrum and vibrate the tiny bones in the middle ear. These vibrations set the fluid in the cochlea in motion, shaking tiny hairs. Nerves attached to the hairs pass the message to the brain.

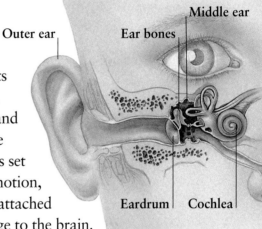

Outer ear

Middle ear

Ear bones

Eardrum Cochlea

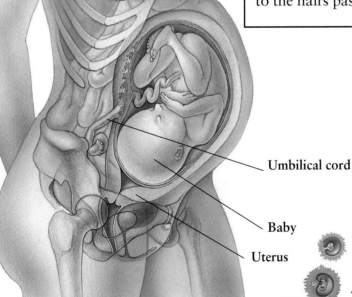

Umbilical cord

Baby

Uterus

2 weeks

4 weeks

6 weeks

8 weeks

Q How does a baby develop during pregnancy?

A A baby's life begins when a male sperm joins a female egg. The sperm travels from a man into a woman's body. It joins with the egg to form a single cell and starts to grow. After a week, the single cell has multiplied to more than one hundred cells. After eight weeks, the baby has all its major organs (such as heart, liver, and lungs). The baby gets its food from its mother through the umbilical cord. After nine months, the baby is about 20 inches (50 cm) long (left). It is ready to be born.

SIMPLE CREATURES

Invertebrates (animals without a backbone) make up 97 percent of all animal species. The weight of all the earthworms, insects, and spiders in the world is many times the weight of its people.

▲ A colorful coral reef grows in shallow water near the coast of Indonesia.

KEY FACTS

Number of species: 1.3–30 million

Largest: Colossal squid, more than 40 feet (12 m) long

Smallest: Many can be seen only through a microscope

A phylum (plural, phyla) is a large group of animals with some features in common. For instance, mammals, birds, reptiles, amphibians, and fish all have a backbone. Together they make up the phylum Chordata.

Most creatures do not have a backbone. They are invertebrates. There are thirty phyla of invertebrates. They are sometimes called simple creatures, but many are not simple.

The invertebrates are an incredibly varied group. Some are aquatic—sponges, jellyfish, corals, sea anemones, octopuses, starfish, and bivalves. Others live mostly in soil—for instance, the annelid worms. Some—like most flatworms—are parasites, living inside other animals. Still more live on plants most of their lives; this is

true for most insects and spiders. Some invertebrates swim, and others walk or fly. And some hardly move at all: They are sedentary.

Arthropods

The phylum Arthropoda is the biggest group of simple creatures, with more than one million species. They range from crabs and lobsters to insects and spiders. Arthropods have a segmented body covered by an external skeleton (exoskeleton). Each body segment usually has one or more pairs of legs attached to it.

Bivalves, gastropods, and octopuses are grouped together in

the phylum Mollusca. There are about eighty-five thousand species. They look very different from each other but share certain features. They usually have a head with

SUPERSIZE SQUID

The largest invertebrates are mollusks called colossal squid. They live at great depths in the Southern Ocean and grow to more than 40 feet (12 m) long. They have the largest eyes of any animal and are the main source of food for sperm whales, which dive to 10,000 feet (3,000 m) to catch them.

► Squid are cephalopods with eight arms and two tentacles. They are strong swimmers and feed on the seabed as well as in the water column. Squid have three hearts.

sensory organs and a muscular foot. And they do not have an internal or external skeleton. A tough, chalky shell often protects them instead.

Sponges, Jellyfish, and Corals

The sponges (phylum Porifera) live on, and are attached to, the shallow ocean floor. They are the simplest animals of all. Some of the five thousand species are very small, but the giant barrel sponge grows to 7.9 feet (2.4 m) in height. The jellyfish, corals, and sea anemones (phylum Cnidaria) form a varied group of 9,500 species. While corals and sea anemones are sedentary creatures, jellyfish drift in ocean currents. Individual corals are small, but they form colonies that can be very large. The tentacles of a lion's mane jellyfish grow up to 120 feet (37 m).

Starfish, Sea Urchins, and Worms

Most starfish, sea urchins, and sea cucumbers (phylum Echinodermata, seven thousand species) have a body arranged into five similar regions around a circular shape. They have lumps of calcium carbonate (called ossicles) embedded in their skin.

GENERAL INFORMATION

● Lesser-known groups of invertebrates include the flatworms (phylum Platyhelminthes, thirteen thousand species), which often live within other animals; roundworms (phylum Nematoda, up to 500,000 species); and the segmented worms (phylum Annelida, nine thousand species).

▲ Lion's mane jellyfish live only in the cold waters of northern oceans.

Q How does a jellyfish sting?

A A jellyfish (right) is a bell-shaped sea animal with its mouth on the underside of its body. Its body is made of two layers of skin with a jellylike layer in between. Long tentacles hang down from the body. The tentacles have stinging cells that the jellyfish uses to stun its prey or protect itself from enemies. Humans can sometimes be hurt by these stings. Inside each stinging cell is a coiled thread (inset). When something touches the cell, the thread shoots out, sticking into the prey and injecting venom. In this way, jellyfish can catch large fish.

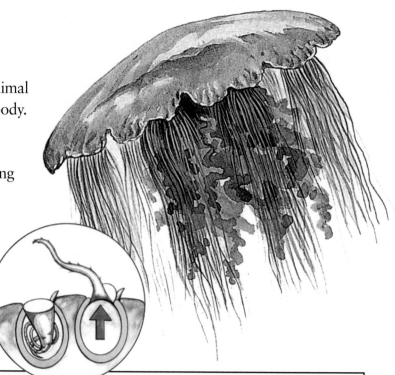

Q A centipede has how many legs?

A A centipede's body is made up of segments. Each segment has one pair of legs attached to it. The centipede in this picture has eighteen segments, and so it has thirty-six legs. Some centipedes have only fifteen segments, and others may have as many as 177 segments.

Q How does an octopus catch its food?

A An octopus (right) has eight tentacles and hunts on the seabed for fish or shellfish. It creeps toward its prey and then pounces, grabbing hold with its tentacles. Suckers on the tentacles hold the prey firmly while the octopus drags it to its mouth.

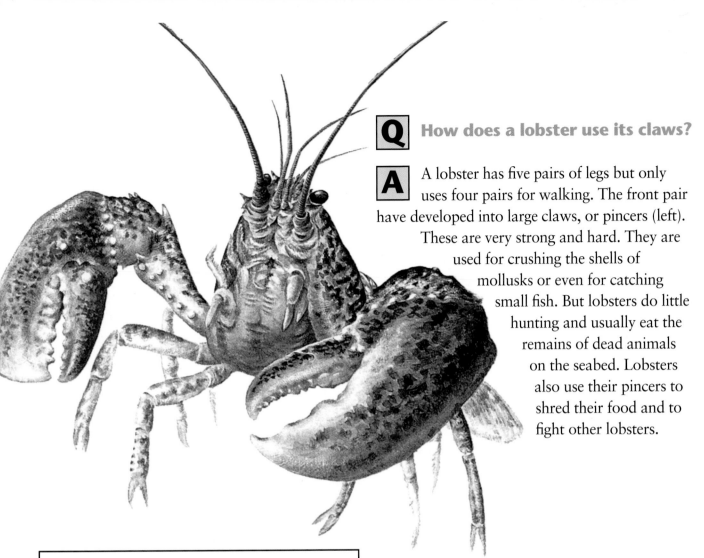

Q How does a lobster use its claws?

A A lobster has five pairs of legs but only uses four pairs for walking. The front pair have developed into large claws, or pincers (left). These are very strong and hard. They are used for crushing the shells of mollusks or even for catching small fish. But lobsters do little hunting and usually eat the remains of dead animals on the seabed. Lobsters also use their pincers to shred their food and to fight other lobsters.

Q How are hermit crabs different from other crabs?

A Hermit crabs have hard shells on their front parts, like other crabs, but their abdomens are soft. They live inside the empty shells of other sea animals for protection.

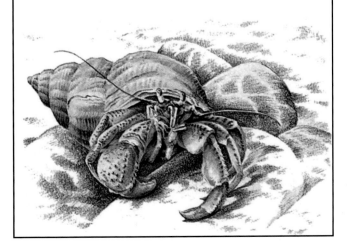

Q Is a starfish really a fish?

A Starfish (below) are not fish but belong to the group of sea animals called echinoderms. The name means "spiny-skinned." Starfish have arms but no head, and no front or back. They move slowly by gripping the seabed with water-filled tubes on their arms. The starfish's arms are so strong that they can pull apart the two shells of a mussel to reach the food inside.

PLANT LIFE

Plants make up the kingdom Plantae, which includes flowering plants, conifers, ferns, mosses, and green algae, but not seaweeds and fungi. Animals could not survive without plants.

Most plants are called vascular plants. They live on land, have a system of leaves, stems, and roots, and have cell walls made of a substance called cellulose. Most get their energy from photosynthesis. That means their leaves use the energy of sunlight to make food.

The root systems of most vascular plants grow in the ground, but some—epiphytes, for instance—grow on other plants. Other vascular plants are parasites: They get their nutrition from the plants that they grow on.

KEY FACTS

Smallest flowering plant: Duckweeds in the genus *Wolffia* are only 0.04–0.08 inches (1–2 mm) across.

Largest flowering plant: A quaking aspen grove in Utah covers 104 acres (43 ha), has forty-seven thousand trunks, and is one genetically identical organism.

Tallest plant: A redwood in California is 380 feet (116 m) tall.

Flowering Plants

About 90 percent of all plants are called angiosperms, or flowering plants. They include daisies, orchids, and broad-leaved trees. A flowering plant usually has roots to anchor it in the soil. These take up water and nutrients. Above ground, a stem carries these to the leaves. The flowers are the reproductive parts of the plant. They produce fruits and seeds when they have been fertilized.

▲ The parts of a flowering plant.

Flower
Seeds
Leaf
Stem
Roots

◀ A bee feeds on a pitcher plant. If the bee falls into the cup, or pitcher, of digestive juices, the plant will digest it.

Nonvascular Plants

Not all plants are vascular. Bryophytes, including mosses and liverworts, for instance, can only survive where moisture is always available. Most remain small throughout their lifetime. Bryophytes do not produce flowers or seeds but instead reproduce by releasing spores.

Plants and Animals

Almost every aspect of animal life depends on plants. Oxygen, which is vital for animals' respiration, is a waste product of plants' photosynthesis. And plants take up carbon dioxide, the buildup of which would be harmful to animals. Plant-eating animals (herbivores) need plants for their food, especially grasses, leaves, and fruits. Meat-eating (carnivorous) animals also depend on plants since they eat the herbivores.

▲ A grove of aspen trees in Utah. Since the root systems of all these trees are connected, this is actually one enormous tree, not many individual ones.

TOXIC PLANTS

Some plants contain toxins (chemicals) that hurt, or even kill, any animals that eat them. Western water hemlock (right) contains the toxin cicutoxin, which attacks animals' central nervous system, causing fits and eventual death.

GENERAL INFORMATION

- At least 300,000 species of plants are known, most of them seed plants and most of them gaining their energy from photosynthesis.

- The first land-living plants that practiced photosynthesis probably evolved around 1,000 million years ago, in the Proterozoic eon.

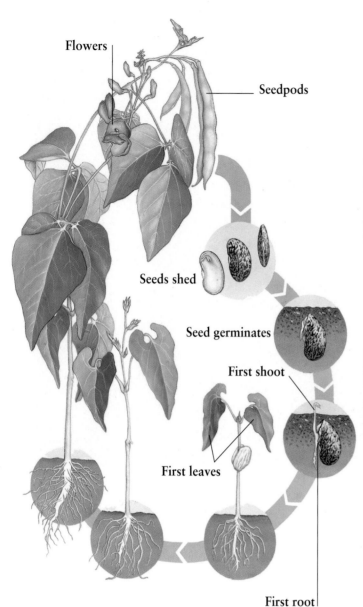

Flowers

Seedpods

Seeds shed

Seed germinates

First shoot

First leaves

First root

Q How can you tell a tree's age?

A Every year, a tree grows a new layer of wood just beneath the bark. If a tree is cut down, the layers can be seen as rings in the cross section through the stump (above). By counting the rings, you can tell the tree's age.

Q Why do plants need sunlight?

A Plants make their own food by combining a gas called carbon dioxide, which they get from the air, with water from the soil. This process is called photosynthesis (below). To power the process, the plant uses the energy of sunlight. A green pigment in the leaves called chlorophyll traps the sun's energy.

Q How does a plant complete its life cycle?

A Every year, plants (above) produce large numbers of seeds, which fall to the ground. Many die but some will germinate. Tiny roots and shoots grow from the seed, and soon the plant increases in size. As the plant grows larger, more and more leaves are produced, and eventually flowers appear. Pollen from male flowers fertilizes female flowers, and the base of the flower begins to swell. It is here that this year's seeds are being made, completing the plant's life cycle.

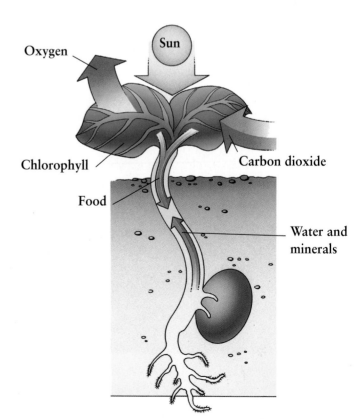

Oxygen

Sun

Chlorophyll

Food

Carbon dioxide

Water and minerals

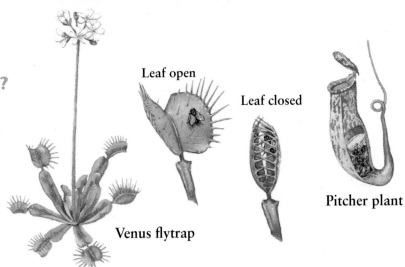

Q Which plants eat animals?

A Venus flytraps and pitcher plants (right) can absorb nutrients from animals. Venus flytraps have leaves that trap insects and digest them. Pitcher plants have flask-shaped leaves in which water collects. Insects fall in, drown, and decay.

Leaf open

Leaf closed

Pitcher plant

Venus flytrap

Q What are fruit pits?

A Fruit pits, or stones, in a plant are the seeds that produced the fruit. There are many types of fruit, and most are juicy and nutritious. Many animals eat the seeds and pits. They may be swallowed whole and passed out in the animal's droppings later on. In this way, the plant has its seeds scattered, or dispersed.

Q Why do plants produce flowers?

A Plants produce flowers (below) to reproduce and create a new generation. Flowers bear the male and female parts. Many flowers have colors and scents that attract insects. The insects take male pollen to the female parts of other flowers. The pollen of some flowers is carried by the wind.

Petal

Pollen

Stigma (female)

Filament

Anther (produces pollen)

Sepal

Ovary (seeds develop here)

Silver birch

Fritillary

Clematis

Orchid

Q How do daffodils survive the winter?

A Daffodils have leaves and flowers above ground only for a few months each spring. During the winter, they live as onionlike bulbs in the ground. The bulbs are full of food and are protected from winter frosts by the soil above them.

Bulb cross section

ECOLOGY

All plants and animals in an area influence each other and their environment, and their environment also influences them. Ecology is the study of these relationships.

Even the smallest area of Earth's surface has many different organisms living on it. All of them affect each other to a greater or lesser degree. Big animals eat small ones. Small animals compete among themselves for food. Even plants compete with each other for valuable light and water.

▲ Road-building projects can block the feeding routes followed by some animals, such as deer. This can harm animal populations.

Food Webs

Food webs are one important aspect of ecology. They show how each living thing gets its food. Plants are

KEY FACTS

Producers: Plants
Primary consumers: Caterpillars, ants, grouse, gazelles, horses
Secondary consumers: Thrushes, mice, porcupines
Tertiary consumers: Hawks, foxes

▼ Killer whales, or orcas, are tertiary consumers. They eat smaller predators such as sea lions. No other animal eats orcas.

called producers. They use light energy from the sun to produce food from carbon dioxide and water. This process is called photosynthesis. Animals are called consumers because—unlike plants—they cannot produce their own food. They have to eat plants, other animals, or both. Animals that eat only plants are herbivores; they are primary consumers. Animals that eat other animals are called carnivores. There are many more herbivores than carnivores.

Different Consumers

Carnivores that eat herbivores are called secondary consumers, and those that eat other carnivores are called tertiary consumers. A killer whale, or orca, is a tertiary consumer, and it is at the top of a food chain that starts with tiny plankton in the ocean. Small fish eat plankton, and then bigger fish eat the small fish. Seals eat the large

AMERICAN BULLFROGS
Introducing an animal to a new place can have a serious effect on its ecology. American bullfrogs were taken to frog farms outside their native North America. They have big appetites. When they escaped, they ate large numbers of endangered fish and amphibians in many parts of the world.

fish, and orcas eat the seals. Nothing eats orcas, so they are at the top of a food chain. Many food chains link up to form a food web.

The Environment

The environment is also important. For example, if pollution kills all the plankton in one area, there will be nothing for the small fish to eat. They will die from starvation and then the bigger fish will also starve, unless they can move to an area

that has not been affected by the pollution. The effects of the pollution will be felt all the way to the top of the food chain.

Geology is another important environmental factor. Plants will grow only if the soil has the right chemical mix for them. The chemical makeup of soil depends on the underlying rocks (bedrock), so plants will grow only in areas with bedrock that suits them. Insects and other herbivores only eat certain plants—so geology affects the animal life of an area.

▲ Large birds called vultures are carrion eaters—they eat mostly animals that have already been killed and part-eaten by predators.

GENERAL INFORMATION

● **Weather and human interference are two important additional elements in an area's ecology.**
● **Ecologists figure out the impact of development on an area's plant and animal life. This is called an environmental impact assessment.**

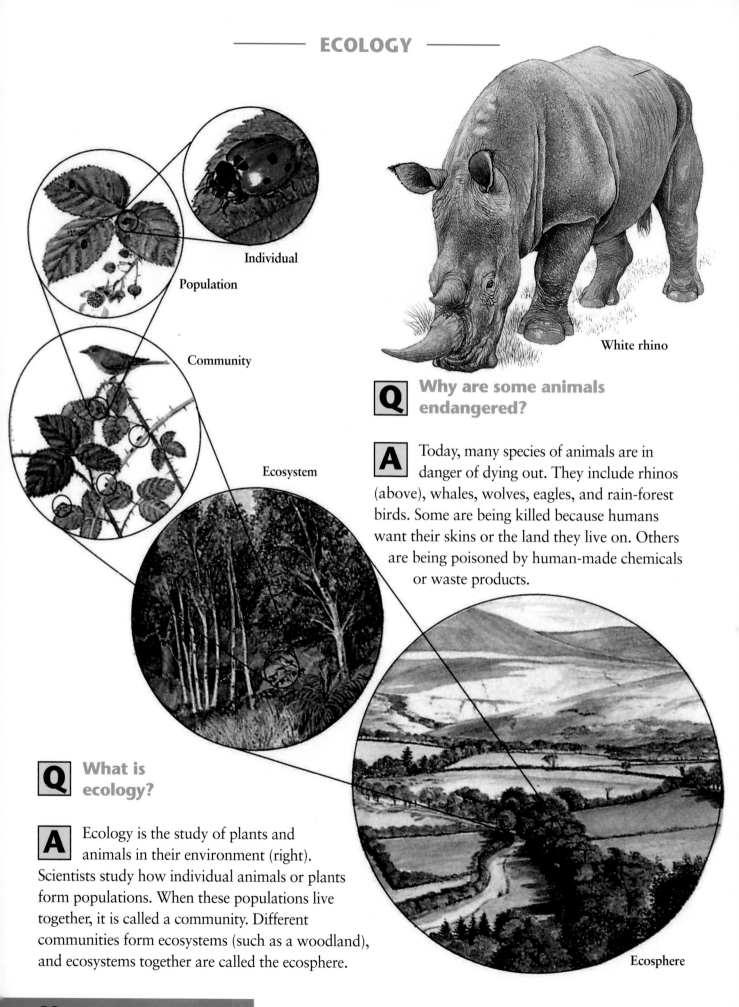

Individual

Population

Community

Ecosystem

White rhino

Q **Why are some animals endangered?**

A Today, many species of animals are in danger of dying out. They include rhinos (above), whales, wolves, eagles, and rain-forest birds. Some are being killed because humans want their skins or the land they live on. Others are being poisoned by human-made chemicals or waste products.

Q **What is ecology?**

A Ecology is the study of plants and animals in their environment (right). Scientists study how individual animals or plants form populations. When these populations live together, it is called a community. Different communities form ecosystems (such as a woodland), and ecosystems together are called the ecosphere.

Ecosphere

28

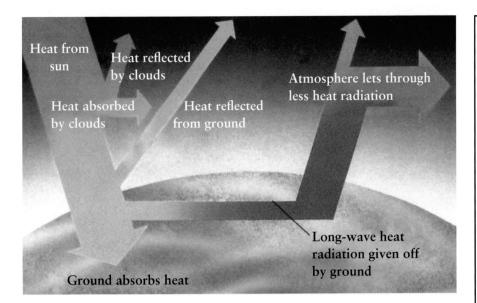

Heat from sun

Heat reflected by clouds

Atmosphere lets through less heat radiation

Heat absorbed by clouds

Heat reflected from ground

Long-wave heat radiation given off by ground

Ground absorbs heat

Q What is the greenhouse effect?

A Heat comes to the Earth from the sun. Most of it is then reflected back into space. But some gases trap the heat inside the Earth's atmosphere, which grows warmer like a greenhouse. This is what is known as the greenhouse effect (above).

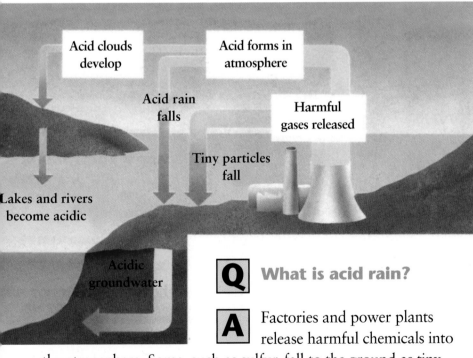

Acid clouds develop

Acid forms in atmosphere

Acid rain falls

Harmful gases released

Tiny particles fall

Lakes and rivers become acidic

Acidic groundwater

Q What is acid rain?

A Factories and power plants release harmful chemicals into the atmosphere. Some, such as sulfur, fall to the ground as tiny particles. The rest are dissolved by the moisture in the atmosphere. When it rains, these chemicals come down, too. This is called acid rain (above). It damages trees and other plants and poisons the soil. Eventually, acid rain drains into rivers and lakes, where it kills many types of fish.

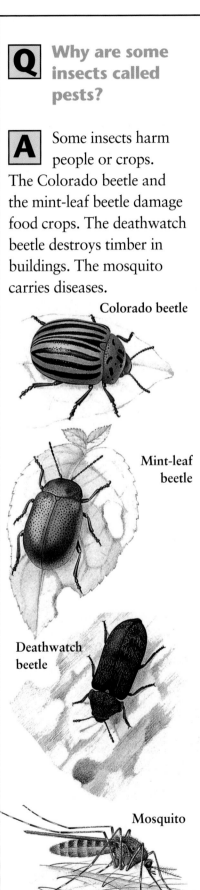

Q Why are some insects called pests?

A Some insects harm people or crops. The Colorado beetle and the mint-leaf beetle damage food crops. The deathwatch beetle destroys timber in buildings. The mosquito carries diseases.

Colorado beetle

Mint-leaf beetle

Deathwatch beetle

Mosquito

GLOSSARY

acid rain Rainfall that has been made acidic by pollution and therefore harmful.

angiosperm A flowering plant.

arthropod An invertebrate such as an insect, spider, or crustacean.

asexual reproduction A type of reproduction where the offspring come from a single parent.

biologist A scientist who studies living organisms—animals or humans.

botanist A scientist who studies plants.

carnivorous An animal (or plant) that feeds on other animals.

consumers Animals and humans are called consumers because they cannot produce food on their own and consume plants, animals, or both. There are primary, secondary, and tertiary consumers.

ecology The study of how humans and animals relate to their environment.

endangered At risk of extinction.

food web A system of interlocking food chains, where each animal depends on another for food.

geology The science that deals with Earth's physical features, such as its structure and rocks, and its history.

global warming The gradual increase in temperature in Earth's atmosphere, which many people believe is caused by pollution.

herbivore An animal that eats only plants.

invertebrate An animal without a backbone, such as a mollusk or annelid.

nonvascular Describes plants that do not draw water up from roots, such as mosses and liverworts.

organism A living thing.

photosynthesis The process by which plants absorb sunlight to make food from carbon dioxide and water.

phylum A large group of animals with features in common. The phylum Chordata includes animals with a backbone: birds, mammals, reptiles, amphibians, and fish.

producers Organisms such as plants that use the sun's energy to produce food.

sexual reproduction A type of reproduction where the offspring come from two parents of different sexes.

vascular Describes plants that draw water up from the ground, and have stems, leaves, and roots, such as flowering plants.

vertebrates Animals that have backbones.

zoologist A scientist who studies animals.

FURTHER READING

Books

Amsel, Sheri. *The Everything KIDS' Human Body Book: All You Need to Know About Your Body Systems—From Head to Toe!*. Avon, MA: Adams Media, 2012.

Burnie, David. *Eyewitness Plant*. DK Eyewitness Books. New York: Dorling Kindersley, 2011.

Dorling Kindersley. *First Human Body Encyclopedia*. New York: DK Children, 2012.

Hague, Bradley. *Alien Deep: Revealing the Mysterious Living World at the Bottom of the Ocean*. Washington, DC: National Geographic Kids, 2012.

Rizzo, Johnna. *Oceans: Dolphins, Sharks, Penguins, and More!*. Washington, DC: National Geographic Kids, 2010.

Websites

Easy Science for Kids: Plants
easyscienceforkids.com/plants
Discover the parts of a plant, how plants reproduce, and the surprising ways in which plants help us in everyday life. Find out how photosynthesis works, and learn all about pollination and fertilization, in this site filled with information and experiments.

Kid's Health: How the Body Works
kidshealth.org/kid/htbw/htbw_main_page.html
Explore all the organs of the human body

through a series of articles and fun videos. Discover how the eyes, ears, nose, and mouth work, and how the digestive system, nervous system, heart, and lungs all keep your body running smoothly.

Neuroscience for Kids
faculty.washington.edu/chudler/chsense.html
Learn all about how the five senses—taste, smell, touch, sight, and hearing—work, and perform experiments to test them at this fun and informative site.

INDEX